Three Elderly Wisemen

Christmas Pageant for Seniors

Judy Gattis Smith

CSS Publishing Company, Inc.
Lima, Ohio

THREE ELDERLY WISEMEN

For more information about CSS Publishing Company resources, visit our website at www.csspub.com, email us at csr@csspub.com, or call (800) 241-4056.

e-book:
ISBN-13: 978-0-7880-2849-6
ISBN-10: 0-7880-2849-9

ISBN-13: 978-0-7880-2848-9
ISBN-10: 0-7880-2848-0

PRINTED IN USA

To Vic, John, and Ed
the three wisemen of
Brandermill Woods Retirement Community

Introduction

Christmas pageants aren't just for children. The wonderful story of Jesus' birth speaks to all ages, and all ages can reenact this traditional celebration.

Biblically only a few verses in the Bible tell of "wisemen from the East" but legends and tradition have given them names: Gaspar, Melchior, and Balthazar and modes of transportation (camels). Some stories make them kings, some astrologers. Times of their arrival differ but, in our churches we usually portray them as part of the traditional manger scene.

This play considers the wisemen as "senior citizens" with the same characteristics as senior citizens today. Melchior is a slave to his daily routine; Gaspar has made many mistakes in his life and is full of regrets; Balthazar has spent his life enjoying every good thing available and is now jaded and cynical. All are healed at the manger.

Cast of Characters

Act I

Narrator
Melchior
Gaspar
Balthazar
Aaliyah (wife of Melchior)
Two servants of Gaspar
Hakum
Doctor (or Balthazar)

Act II

The three wisemen

Act III

Mary and Joseph and baby Jesus and as many characters as you wish to include in a traditional manger scene or a backdrop of this scene

Setting

This play is presented in three acts. In Act I the wisemen are getting ready for the long journey to Bethlehem. If a stage and lighting are available, all three wisemen could be on the stage at the beginning, each on a separate section of the stage. A spotlight could focus in turn on each of the wisemen as he begins his preparation for the journey to Bethlehem.

In Act II the wisemen are together and on their journey. An outdoor setting with a backdrop of Herod's palace in the distance would be appropriate.

The setting for Act III is the traditional manger scene. Perhaps you might want to copy the pose on a favorite Christmas card with Mary and Joseph and the baby plus shepherds and townsfolk.

The final scene, Postlude, could be the same as Act I with all three wisemen present on the stage, each spotlighted in turn.

This play could also be done as a readers' theater without costumes, props, or scenery. The Narrator would set the scene, inviting the audience to use their imaginations.

Three Elderly Wisemen

Welcome

Scripture
Matthew 2: 1-12

Characters
Narrator
Aaliyah — Melchior's wife
Melchior

Narrator
Preparations are being made for a journey in three far-away kingdoms.

Act I, Scene 1
Melchior

Aaliyah: Here is your medicine dear, right on schedule. Why, what are you doing? It looks like you are packing.

Melchior: I am going on a journey.

Aaliyah: A journey? Why? How long will you be gone? It's really not the best time of year for a journey.

Melchior: Yes, I'm leaving tonight and I'm really not sure how long I'll be gone.

Aaliyah: Leaving tonight? But this is ridiculous. You are always in bed by 9:00. You know how you need your sleep. What on earth is this all about?

Melchior: It's a star — a strange star in the sky — a moving star of unusual brightness. I must follow it.

Aaliyah: But this is so unlike you. If there is one thing about you, it's that you are sensible. And this certainly is not sensible. You know how you always get up at the same time every morning, eat the same thing for breakfast, read the latest news, keep your routine going.

Melchior: Maybe it's time I changed.

Aaliyah: Here, let me feel your head. Do you have a fever?

Melchior: I'm fine really. It's just that I must go.

Aaliyah: Who will look after you? Who will get your medicine to you — see that your meals are served right on time? How will you get your food? I'll go with you.

Melchior: It's all right, I'll take Abdul. You know what a trustworthy servant he is. He'll look after me. Don't worry. You stay here where it is safe.

Aaliyah: Safe? You mean you are going where it is dangerous?

Melchior: I'm not sure. I'm not sure where the star will lead me.

Aaliyah: Dear, consider your age. As long as you stay on your schedule, you are healthy. You've always kept to your routine.

Melchior: And lived only in my own personal little world. I've walked the same path, followed the same schedule, eaten the same food, talked to the same people, had the same conversation over and over. I've become frozen in place.

Aaliyah: So, what is wrong with that?

Melchior: I just have the feeling now that there is so much more. And I have the opportunity to explore it. This star... this star.

Aaliyah: If there is a star that must be followed, let someone younger go. You know how often you have said the young people are in charge of the world now. We're obsolete. Let *them* follow this star.

Melchior: No! This is *my* quest. The young cannot possibly understand what this means.

Aaliyah: You frighten me. I fear senility has set in. You've always kept on your schedule and always met your deadlines. Now you are talking about a journey you are not sure where you are going to, or how long you will be gone. I'm going to call the doctor right now.

Melchior: No! Please understand. Some great mystery has appeared in my neatly scheduled life. I see a new world — unprecedented possibilities. I'll return but for now I must go. (*Melchior leaves*)

Aaliyah: Please be careful. I'll be waiting for you.

Act I, Scene 2

Gaspar

Characters
Gaspar
Servant 1 and Servant 2
Hakum — Grand Vizier

Narrator: In another city another king is making preparations.

Gaspar: Hurry up with those things! Where are those lazy servants?

(*servants whisper to each other*)

Servant 1: Sounds like it is going to be one of *those* days.

Servant 2: Is he planning another journey?

Servant 1: Seems like it.

Servant 2: I wonder where he'll go this time?

Servant 1: Probably another of his get-rich quick schemes.

Servant 2: And someone will suffer for it.

Gaspar: What are you two whispering about? Have you got everything? You know what I need. What's taking you so long? Let's see a little hustle. And send in my Grand Vizier!

Servants together: Yes, oh king!

(*servants exit*)

(*Hakum enters and bows*)

Gaspar: I'm going on a journey. My kingdom is in order. You know where everything is. I expect you to keep my kingdom running while I am away — until I return.

Hakum: Yes, oh king.

Gaspar: (*to himself*) Not that anyone cares if I return or not.

Hakum: May I ask where you are going?

Gaspar: I am following a strange new, unusually bright star in the sky. My wisemen tell me it is of great importance — that it announces the birth of a new king. Perhaps I can expand my kingdom.

Hakum: (*clearing his throat*) May I remind you of other stars you have followed in the past and the resulting consequences?

Gaspar: You mean those stars that led me into battle? Yes, and you alone know how much I regret those — the lost lives — the bloody conquests — the senseless destruction. I was young and ambitious. They were a mistake and I regret them still. I wake up at night and recall those bloody scenes and hear those screams.

Hakum: And Queen Aisha?

Gaspar: Another false path. Another mistaken star. Sometimes I am overwhelmed with what I have missed. I could have shared my kingdom with *her*. I could have known love and a family — a son. (*silence*) You alone have stood by me through all my mistakes.

Hakum: When I was young, I pledged to serve you. I have also tried to be a friend.

Gaspar: I thought Jabara was my friend. I thought he was the star I could follow. His betrayal is still a pain in my life. The pain seems to grow stronger every year. I had to have him killed, but sometimes I wish the knife had plunged in me. Oh Hakum, I have made so many mistakes, gone down so many wrong paths. I wish I could live my life over.

Hakum: And yet, you embark on another journey?

Gaspar: I have to. I don't want all these past mistakes to define my entire life. There is so much about my life that I have to come to terms with. I need time to sort out all these mistakes — air them —. Following this star will give me time to ponder if I have learned anything from them.

Hakum: But you could do that here.

Gaspar: No there is something about the power in that star. I feel it will help me resolve these mistakes I have made in my life. Maybe all these side roads were not merely wasted. If I can find where that star leads, I shall find the answer I have sought my *entire* life. Not just for myself but others. I once had dreams — then all the glories and sad mistakes. I want to start over, to right these wrongs. I want to dream again. I am going to follow this star.

Act I, Scene 3

Balthazar
(*King Balthazar and his personal doctor*)

Narrator: A third king is visiting his doctor in preparation for his journey.

Balthazar: I want to stock up on that pain medicine you gave me and some potions for sleeping and some of that salve for my leg. I am going on a journey.

15

Doctor: A journey? I really can't recommend this, not at your age and in your condition. Why take chances? You have everything you need here. Your health is fragile.

Balthazar: This is something I want to do. A strange new star has appeared in the sky. I want to follow it.

Doctor: But you have already been everywhere, seen everything there is to see, met all the important rulers.

Balthazar: And it all bored me to death.

Doctor: Strange food may upset your delicate stomach — make your condition worse.

Balthazar: Food no longer interests me. I have tasted the finest the world has to offer. I can't even taste anymore.

Doctor: Well, I'll admit, it is good to see you interested in something again. You have been quite depressed lately. Do you think the new medicine is helping?

Balthazar: It has nothing to do with medicine.

Doctor: The last time I saw you, you said you were ready to give up on life. "None of it was worth the effort," you said. Remember, I offered several things to keep up your spirits and take your mind off your pain.

Balthazar: Bah! Actors — music — dancing girls — games. None hold my interest for long. I feel nothing. I am cold and unresponsive. But this star — it is so *unusual*. Neither my wise men nor myself have ever seen anything like it. It seems to beckon me to follow.

Doctor: Hmm. How far do you plan to go, and how will you travel?

Balthazar: Probably by camel. I don't know how far.

Doctor: Camel? No, no. Your leg would be killing you within an hour. Can't you arrange for a litter to carry you? Perhaps you could cushion it with velvets and draw drapes against the scorching sun.

Balthazar: I'll travel by night as I must have a clear view of the sky.

Doctor: Of course I can't accompany you but I *can* give you the names of good doctors in every direction. They will be glad to treat you. They are expensive, but I know you have the money to pay.

Balthazar: Thank you, but I'm traveling light and I don't want to stop or have someone who might slow me down.

Doctor: As your doctor I can't condone this journey. I can keep you comfortable here.

Balthazar: What? And just wait for death? Sometimes I feel I am already dead — just withering away. This star points to joy and I haven't experienced joy in a long time!

Act II, Scene 1

Narrator: Along the way the three journeys crossed paths and rather than a solitary trek, the kings began to journey together.

(*one night around a campfire*)

Melchior: The star is unusually beautiful tonight, is it not?

(*other kings nod agreement*)

Balthazar: What does it mean, do you think?

Gaspar: Aren't we all agreed from our studies, that the star portends the birth of a great king?

Melchior: Yes, according to my astrologers, nothing like it has *ever* been seen before. A star that moves across the sky, with rays reaching down to us here — guiding us — leading us — as bright as the sun and moon together.

Balthazar: We'll soon be near the palace of that great king, Herod. I met him once. He likes to keep up with everything going on in his kingdom. He could probably direct us to the birthplace of this new king. Perhaps it is there, inside Herod's palace that we will find the new baby. We may be near the end of our journey.

Gaspar: So you've met him — this Herod. What's he like?

Balthazar: To be honest, I'm not sure. He is hard to read. Brilliant, certainly, but cunning like a fox. He'll be impressed with our knowledge.

Melchior: Should we present our gifts to him, do you think?

Balthazar: Let's wait and see. I have money to bribe the inner circle surrounding Herod. Let's keep our gifts for the new king.

Melchior: What did you bring anyway? Something smells wonderful.

Balthazar: That's probably my gift — myrrh. It comes from the southern most area of my kingdom in the Arabian Peninsula. It is used in all perfumes, also in cosmetics and ointments.

Gaspar: How did you decide on that as a gift?

Balthazar: It's a valuable gift in my country but it has a personal association for me. It's also for pain — a wonderful release when mixed with wine.

Melchior: Is some in that salve you put on your leg? Is that what we smell?

Balthazar: There is some myrrh in that mixture but the jar I am giving the new king is myrrh in its purest form — the form used in preparing a corpse for burial. A strange gift you may think. (*pause*) This new king represents new birth to me.

I was dead to things of the world. I can buy or obtain anything I want, but these are only expensive toys with which I try to fill the emptiness inside me. Stirring now, since I have been following this star, is a world of wonder and insight. I am beginning to understand that I have, have always had, enough. Now I'm tasting the essence of life itself, not the accessories. This new king represents new life to me — the death of my old way of life. Strange that it comes now when my physical death is so near. Enough about me. What did you bring?

Gaspar: My gift also has a personal meaning. I bring frankincense. Its main use in my country is for treating bleeding wounds and bruises. I have so many in my life — not just physical wounds but wounds and bruises far deeper. I believe that I shall be healed when I present this gift to the new king — healed and forgiven. I have the feeling that this new king may also have need of balm in his life — that he will be a healer as well as a king.

Melchior: My gift is less creative. I bring gold, the universal gift of choice. But with this gift I hope to open worlds of possibilities to the new king. I hope he will use it to create something new or perhaps it can be a part of his crown.

Gaspar: Look! The star is moving again. Let's be on our way.

Act II, Scene 2

Narrator: The three kings did arrive at Herod's palace, but the reception was not what they expected. Now they are on their journey again just leaving the palace grounds.

Balthazar: It is certainly a great palace where Herod lives — but not as great as I remember from earlier days.

Melchior: We were treated well though.

Gaspar: But Herod seemed surprised at our news. Oh, he tried to hide his feelings but it was obvious to me that he knew nothing about this new king.

Balthazar: I got that feeling too. And even the servants that I bribed for information seemed to know nothing.

Gaspar: Yes, but the prophets did — those wise men Herod summoned. Did you see how they glanced at each other? They knew something all right.

Melchior: You'd think these people would be so happy that God had at last sent to them the king that God had promised.

Gaspar: Could we have been wrong? We come to welcome and worship the Savior of the world — all the way from the East — all this long journey. Yet here at the seat of power, they know nothing.

Melchior: The best scholars of all three of our kingdoms could not have all been wrong. And don't forget the star. It seemed to speak to all of us with great power.

Gaspar: We certainly had to wait a long time while Herod conferred with those priests and scribes.

Balthazar: They were studying ancient scrolls that prophets had written long ago — to find out where this long prophesied king would be born.

Gaspar: If he was to be born. When they finally decided on Bethlehem as the birthplace, I wondered if they were just trying to get rid of us — just save their own skins by producing a location. I think Herod suspected that they really didn't know either, or else I think he would have come with us.

Melchior: He did tell us to come back to the palace and let him know when we found the child so he could come and worship him.

Gaspar: But we could all see how phoney that was — urging us to hurry to Bethlehem and search diligently for the child. Then he dismissed us without another word. He obviously was ready for us to move on.

Balthazar: Yes, he had our camels all ready for mounting. The road to Bethlehem was pointed out to us, but now there is little daylight left. Perhaps we should stay another night.

Melchior: Let's be on our way. I'm anxious to get out of here. "South" Herod said, "and not too far."

(after Melchoir speaks, stagehands create loud bang)

Gaspar: Did you hear that bang? The great gates to the city just closed behind us. We are on our own again. Herod didn't even send soldiers to accompany us.

Balthazar: Look there it is — the star again and it is moving!

Melchior: We are not wrong. The ever-approaching mystical light goes before us.

Gaspar: We will find this new king — this Savior of the world.

Act III, Scene 1

(at the manger)

Gaspar: Can this be the place?

Melchior: The star has stopped moving and the rays seem brighter than ever. They look like a shining path leading from heaven — straight down to this place.

Gaspar: It looks like a stable — but it has been transformed.

Balthazar: And listen to that sound. I have heard great music but nothing like this. What sweetness is in that song! It fills me with joy!

Gaspar: Quick, let's gather our gifts. Let's enter. There are no barriers here — no one to stop us or question us. No swords are drawn against us.

Balthazar: Dust off my cape! Polish my crown! Help me stand straight! I am going into the presence of royalty now.

Melchior: The light inside almost blinds me. And what is this scene I see spotlighted before me? It is like a beautiful tableau: a young mother, a proud father and a new baby. This is a common enough scene, and yet it is glorified. What beauty I see in the commonplace — the ordinary.

Gaspar: Who are all these people? Why are they here? They look like the simple people that serve me. But they are accepted here as equals. Even women are here. How strange. Do I sense a new way to rule? This is the Savior of the world. That makes him my Savior too.

Balthazar: They are opening up a path for us straight to the manger. Can someone help me? I want to present my gift.

Gaspar: Here, I'll help you. Lean on me.

(*wisemen present gifts here, one at a time*)

Balthazar: Myrrh loses its fragrance here. Here, there is a sweet smell. Perhaps it is the freshness of the hay — an aroma like spring in the meadows — like newness.

Gaspar: Yes, I sense that freshness too — that newness. Here I lay my frankincense down and I feel new. That baby represents a beginning — not just of his life but for all of us.

Melchior: What a surprise that we find the king here — not in a palace — not where we expected him at all. And my gift, gold, loses its gleam beneath this heavenly light. It looks tarnished and dull. The finest and best in my kingdom, the traditional great gift, is nothing. Nothing is as I expected it. My world is turned upside down.

Gaspar: All ages are here too. Look at that boy who presented a lamb to the mother. What a regal carriage he has! He can't be more than ten years old — like the son I never had.

Melchior: The mother accepts all gifts equally. Some women have brought cakes, still warm from the oven. I always just accepted cakes like these as part of my daily food. But now, sitting right beside my gold, even that seems transformed.

Balthazar: I am feeling very tired now. Let's rest here tonight instead of going back to the palace.

Gaspar: Yes, I have no desire for satin sheets tonight.

(*Narrator invites congregation to sing "Joy To The World"*)

Act II, Scene 2

Narrator: It is now the next morning.

Melchior: I had the strangest dream last night.

Gaspar: I also dreamed and it was not my usual nightmare.

Melchior: It was as if an angel spoke directly to me and warned me not to return to Herod and the palace.

Gaspar: That was the feeling in my dream. All those suspicions we felt at the palace were affirmed and I felt that I must not go back there.

Melchior: I am very anxious to go home now. I have no desire to linger anywhere.

Gaspar: I wonder if there is another way to return that doesn't go by the palace? We no longer have the star to guide us.

Melchior: My servant knows a different way to return — a shortcut. I'm so anxious to get back to Aaliyah and tell her all that has happened. I'm leaving now.

Gaspar: I also will leave as soon as my camel and servants are ready.

(*Balthazar enters; Melchoir leaves*)

Balthazar: I am not going back to the palace. You can take the message to Herod. I don't have the energy or desire to see Herod again.

Gaspar: We feel the same. Melchior is already mounted and ready to go. I also am anxious to leave.

Balthazar: So here we part. It has been an incredible journey. You have been great traveling companions.

Postlude

Narrator: And so the three kings begin their long journey home, each by a separate way. As they travel, they ponder what the journey has meant to them.

Melchior: What an incredible journey this has been. I have discovered how wonderful life is. There are unbelievable surprises awaiting me every day. They were there, where I lived, all along. I just let daily life get in my way. I look forward to returning home, but I will never be imprisoned by routine again. My eyes have been opened. How can I think there is a sameness to our days or that I am in control? My old formulas are shattered. Something new is born every day, and I will watch for it eagerly and carefully.

Gaspar: I am forgiven. I see life differently now. All that has happened to me — all the wrong paths I have taken were not lost. They all taught me great lessons. Violence is never the answer — love is, kindness is, and none of us is perfect.

We all make mistakes. I have been haughty and arrogant. I'm only a part of a great universe, not the center of it. Now I have another chance. I will rule more lovingly. I will forgive and accept others, *all* others.

Balthazar: Finally the empty place inside me is filled. It is not "things" that satisfy me but the presence of God in my life. I know great peace now, and a joy far greater than I could ever imagine. I feel immersed in the great mystery of life. Being alive with God is the greatest gift of all. I probably will not survive the long journey back to my home, but it is of no concern. My search has ended. And I have the assurance that the presence of God I now feel in my life will not desert me in death.

Narrator: To end our story, please join together to sing "We Three Kings."

Other Judy Gattis Smith CSS Titles

Let the Children Come and Worship

NEED info to make this page look as others: isbn, price

Teaching the Mystery of God to Children

A Christmas Journey

It's So Christmas-See!

www.ingramcontent.com/pod-product-compliance
Lightning Source LLC
Chambersburg PA
CBHW071808020426
42331CB00008B/2439